BLOODAXE POETRY
INTRODUCTIONS: 1

Books by Neil Astley

ANTHOLOGIES

Staying Alive: real poems for unreal times
(Bloodaxe Books, 2002; Miramax Books, USA, 2003)
Pleased to See Me: 69 very sexy poems (Bloodaxe Books, 2002)
Do Not Go Gentle: poems for funerals (Bloodaxe Books, 2003)
Being Alive: the sequel to Staying Alive (Bloodaxe Books, 2004)
Passionfood: 100 Love Poems (Bloodaxe Books, 2005)

BLOODAXE POETRY INTRODUCTIONS

1: *Elizabeth Alexander, Moniza Alvi,
   Imtiaz Dharker, Jackie Kay* (2006)
2: *Hans Magnus Enzensberger, Miroslav Holub,
   Marin Sorescu, Tomas Tranströmer* (2006)
FURTHER TITLES TO BE ANNOUNCED

NOVELS

The End of My Tether (Flambard Press, 2002; Scribner, 2003)
The Sheep Who Changed the World (Flambard Press, 2005)